CORAL
Reef Builders

Lynn George

PowerKiDS
press
New York

Published in 2011 by The Rosen Publishing Group, Inc.
29 East 21st Street, New York, NY 10010

First Edition

Editor: Joanne Randolph
Book Design: Kate Laczynski
Photo Researcher: Jessica Gerweck

Photo Credits: Cover, pp. 1, 4, 6 (right), 7, 8,12–13, 15, 18, 19, 20 (right), 22 Shutterstock.com; back cover and interior blueprint © www.iStockphoto.com/Branko Miokovic; p. 5 David Fleetham/Getty Images; p. 6 (left) Reinhard Dirscherl/Getty Images; p. 9 © www.iStockphoto.com/63alfred; p. 10 Robert F. Sisson/ National Geographic/Getty Images; p. 11 © J. W. Alker/age fotostock; p. 14 (left) Mohamed Abdulla Shafeeg/Getty Images; p. 14 (right) © www.iStockphoto.com/Simon Parker; p. 16 (hard hat) © www. iStockphoto.com/Don Nichols; pp. 16–17 (background) © www.iStockphoto.com/Krzysztof Odziomek; p. 20 (left) Alex Kerstitch/Getty Images; p. 21 David Wrobel/Getty Images.

Library of Congress Cataloging-in-Publication Data

George, Lynn.
  Coral : reef builders / Lynn George. — 1st ed.
      p. cm. — (Animal architects)
  Includes index.
  ISBN 978-1-4488-0694-2 (library binding) — ISBN 978-1-4488-1349-0 (pbk.) —
ISBN 978-1-4488-1350-6 (6-pack)
  1. Corals—Juvenile literature. 2. Coral reef ecology—Juvenile literature. 3. Coral reefs and islands—Juvenile literature. I. Title.
  QL377.C5G46 2011
  593.6—dc22
                                2010005273

Manufactured in the United States of America

CPSIA Compliance Information: Batch #WS10PK: For Further Information contact Rosen Publishing, New York, New York at 1-800-237-9932

CONTENTS

WHAT IS A CORAL POLYP?

Does the word "coral" make you think of rocklike hills and walls in the ocean? If it does, you might be surprised to learn that corals are not rocks. Corals are small ocean animals!

A single coral is called a **polyp**. There are many kinds of corals. Stony corals are the best known. They have soft bodies but

Corals and the reefs they build can be beautiful, colorful places, as this one shown here is.

make hard outer **skeletons** for themselves. As stony corals die, they leave their skeletons behind. New corals then grow on top of these skeletons. Over time this forms coral reefs, which are home to lots of ocean animals. Thousands and thousands of corals may make up a single reef!

KINDS OF CORALS

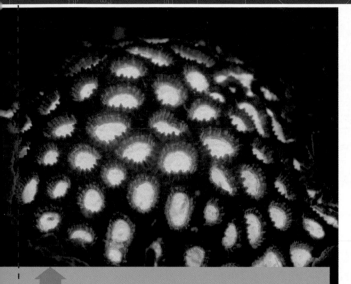

Corals have matter in their bodies that gives off light like this when a special light is shined on them at night.

Brain coral gets its name because it grows in a rounded shape and is covered in lots of grooves, which makes it look like a brain.

There are more than 2,000 **species** of corals. Most corals live in **colonies**. Some corals are soft. They have hardened body parts inside their bodies but do not make outer shells. Their colonies are shaped like plates, fingers, fans, or bushes. They can be yellow, rose, purple, brown, or black.

Some corals, such as stony corals, are hard. They have outer skeletons. They may be dull yellow, brown, or green. Brain, star, rock, and staghorn coral are hard. What shapes do you

think go with these names?

It is these hard corals that are the **architects** of coral reefs. Most kinds of reef-building corals like to live in **tropical** waters. Some corals build reefs in cold water, though.

CORAL UP CLOSE

You have to look really closely to see a coral polyp. Reefs can be miles (km) long, but most polyps are less than 1 inch (2.5 cm) across!

A polyp's shape is almost plantlike. Its tube-shaped body is like a stem. The **tentacles** circling the mouth at the top look like a flower. Stingers

The brain coral shown here sends out its tentacles to find food each night. The tentacles are the clear parts you can see here. Facing page: *This is a close-up look at a stony coral polyp called* Blastomussa wellsi.

cover the tentacles. The polyp uses its tentacles to guard itself from enemies and gather food.

A polyp gets food from special **algae** living inside it, which is like the way plants make food. These tiny algae have a big name. They are called zooxanthellae (zoh-uh-zan-THEH-lee).

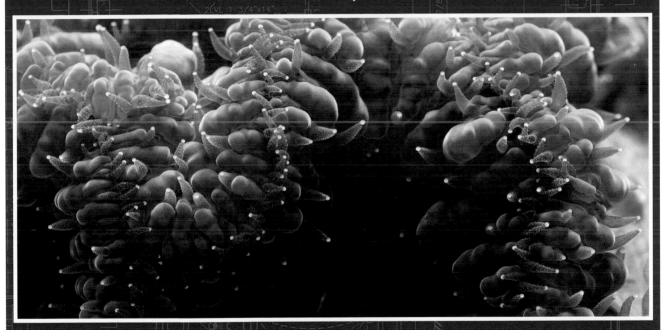

These algae help the coral do another big job. They help the coral use **calcium** it takes from the ocean to build its skeleton.

A LOOK AT A CORAL'S LIFE

You might wonder how this strange, plantlike animal makes new polyps. It has two ways. One way is by producing eggs, just as other animals do. Each egg grows into a **larva** that looks like a tiny jellyfish. This larva swims away. After a while, it falls to the ocean floor and fixes itself to something hard, such as a reef or rock. It changes

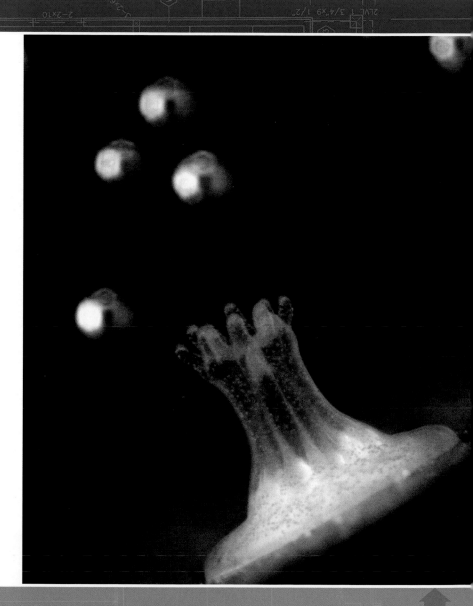

This coral larva has fixed itself to something. It has grown a tube-shaped body and 12 tentacles.

A colony such as this one grows from budding polyps. As each bud grows into a polyp, it in turn makes its own buds.

into a polyp, and a new colony begins.

Polyps also make new polyps through budding, just as some plants make new plants from budding. Small buds appear on an adult polyp's body. When a bud gets large enough, it separates and forms its own skeleton. Budding is how a colony grows larger.

BUILDING A CORAL REEF

Would you believe that a huge reef begins with a single polyp? It buds, then each new polyp forms buds, too. Those polyps, in turn, make more new polyps. They have formed a coral colony! Different colonies that are close together will combine. **Layers** build up as corals die, and more corals grow and bud atop their skeletons.

This reef has likely been growing for a long time. As the reef grows larger, it can support more life.

Reefs form mostly in warm ocean water. The water must be **shallow** so sunlight can reach the polyps. The algae inside the polyps need sunlight to make food.

Reefs grow very slowly. They may grow less than 1 inch (2.5 cm) a year. It may take millions of years to form a huge reef!

DIFFERENT SORTS OF CORAL REEFS

This is a fringing reef in Maldives. The corals grow right along the shore around the island.

This coral atoll is in the Indian Ocean. Note its ring shape.

Every reef is the same, right? That is not true. Three main types of coral reefs exist. These are fringing reefs, barrier reefs, and atolls.

Fringing reefs are the most common. They form along coastlines and follow the shape of the coast. In fact, a fringing reef grows out directly

from the shore. Barrier reefs are much like fringing reefs except they are farther from shore. A **lagoon** separates this kind of reef from the shore. Atolls are ring-shaped reefs that surround a central lagoon.

Some scientists name a fourth type of reef, called a patch reef. Patch reefs are small reefs that are not part of a larger reef system.

PARTS OF A CORAL REEF

1 The coral reef is not made up only of the coral **structures** themselves. The lagoon, which is the water between the shore and the highest part of the reef, is one part of a coral reef. It may be thin or wide. It may be shallow or deep.

5 The outer part of the reef drops very steeply, like a cliff. This is the seaward slope, or deep fore reef. Together, the buttress zone and seaward slope form the fore reef zone.

2 The part where the bottom of the lagoon rises toward the highest part of the reef is called the back reef. The lagoon and back reef together make the reef flat.

3 The highest part of the reef is the reef crest, or algal ridge. When the tide is low, this part sticks out of the water.

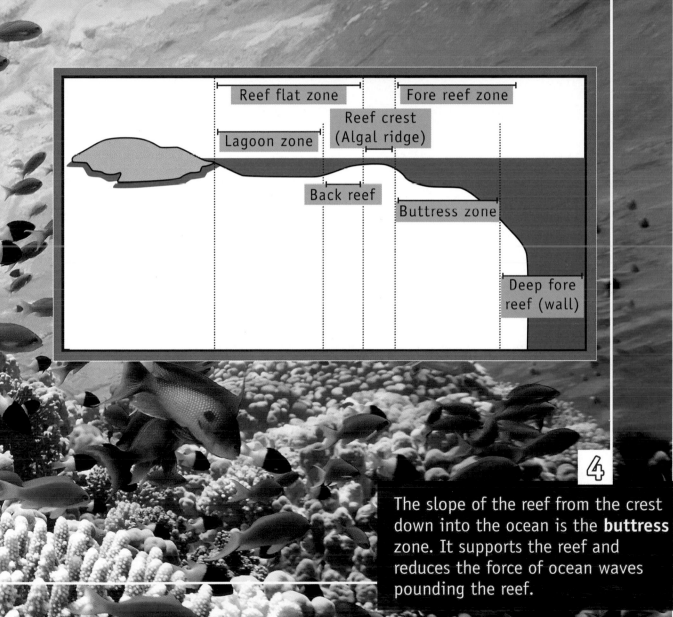

Reef flat zone

Fore reef zone

Reef crest
(Algal ridge)

Lagoon zone

Back reef

Buttress zone

Deep fore
reef (wall)

4 The slope of the reef from the crest down into the ocean is the **buttress** zone. It supports the reef and reduces the force of ocean waves pounding the reef.

A COLORFUL, CROWDED CORAL REEF

Brightly colored parrot fish, such as this one and the one on the facing page, live in the coral reef ecosystem. Their front teeth form a kind of beak!

Here you can see corals and lots of colorful fish. All the plants and animals in the reef play a part in keeping their ecosystem healthy.

Imagine a crowded, colorful city. Imagine a rain forest, made up of many layers of plants and animals. A reef is something like both of those things. Polyps build these structures that make homes for tens of thousands of animal species. There are plants in the reef **ecosystem**, too.

Reefs are busy places! There are animals that hide under the sand at the bottom of the reef. Some fix themselves to the reef itself. Still others swim in the waters around the reef. Reef animals include colorful clown fish, butterfly fish, angelfish, clams, crabs, octopuses, sponges, and starfish. There are eels, sea turtles, sea snakes, and

sharks, too. The main plants are sea grasses. There are different kinds of seaweeds, too, but these are really large algae.

AUSTRALIA'S AWESOME GREAT BARRIER REEF

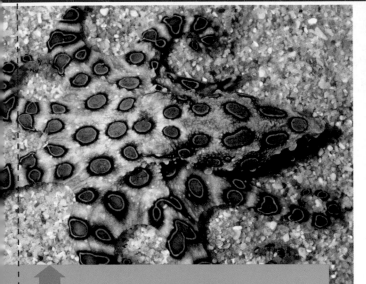

The blue-ringed octopus is only about the size of a golf ball, but there is enough poison in one bite from this animal to kill 26 people!

Great white sharks live in cooler waters throughout the world's oceans. In Australia, these sharks hunt off the southern coast.

Have you heard of Australia's Great Barrier Reef? It is the world's best-known coral reef. It is also the world's biggest reef. It is about 1,400 miles (2,300 km) long. The Great Barrier Reef is actually made up of about 3,000 individual reefs. Can you believe that just one or two polyps likely started these reefs millions of years ago?

The reef is home to a huge number of animal species. These include about 400 coral species, 1,500 fish species, and 14 sea snake species. Giant clams more than 3 feet

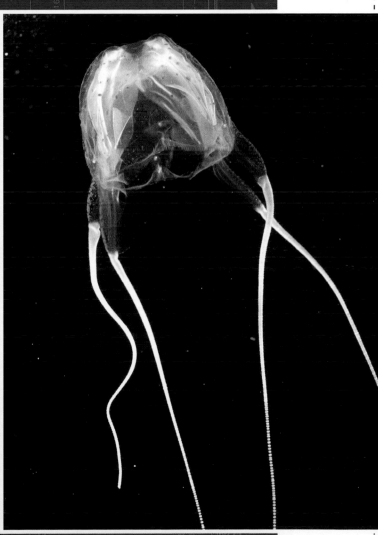

(1 m) long can be found there, too. Some of the world's deadliest animals live in this reef. The box jellyfish, the blue-ringed octopus, the stonefish, and the great white shark are just a few of them!

TAKING CARE OF CORAL REEFS

Coral reefs are beautiful and important places. They supply homes and food to countless animal species. Coral reefs keep coasts safe from ocean waves and storms. The animals that live there supply food and medicine for people, too.

Today, coral reefs face many dangers. Oceans are getting warmer and hurting the polyps that build the reefs. People hurt reefs, too. Boats dirty the water, killing polyps, fish, and other animals. People catch too many fish, and they swim in reefs and break off pieces of coral. People must work together to take care of coral reefs.

GLOSSARY

algae (AL-jee) Plantlike living things without roots or stems that live in water.

architects (AHR-kuh-tekts) People who have ideas and make plans for buildings.

buttress (BUH-tres) A structure that sticks out from another structure and gives it support.

calcium (KAL-see-um) A silverish white metal that makes bones and teeth strong.

colonies (KAH-luh-neez) A group of animals of the same species living close together.

ecosystem (EE-koh-sis-tem) A community of living things and the surroundings in which they live.

lagoon (luh-GOON) The water between the shore and a coral reef.

larva (LAHR-vuh) An animal in an early period of life in which it looks different from the adult form of the animal.

layers (LAY-erz) Individual thicknesses of something.

polyp (PAH-lip) The name for a single coral animal.

shallow (SHA-loh) Not deep.

skeletons (SKEH-leh-tunz) What give animals' or people's bodies shape.

species (SPEE-sheez) A single kind of living thing. All people are one species.

structures (STRUK-cherz) Forms or buildings.

tentacles (TEN-tih-kulz) Long, thin growths on animals that are used to touch, hold, or move.

tropical (TRAH-puh-kul) Warm year-round.

23

INDEX

WEB SITES

Due to the changing nature of Internet links, PowerKids Press has developed an online list of Web sites related to the subject of this book. This site is updated regularly. Please use this link to access the list:

www.powerkidslinks.com/arch/coral/